Underbelly

— Poems —

Malena Spar

Malenaspar.com

Edited by Megan Febuary
Illustrated by Ifrah Fatima
Designed by Charlyn Samson

ISBN: 979-8-218-07103-5 (paperback)
ISBN: 979-8-218-07104-2 (ebook)
Library of Congress Control Number: 2022916756

To my little one, may you be free

Contents

Darkness

How do you feel?
my dream asked

Unmoored, estranged
I replied

I've done everything right
By others
To lead to this moment

But now
Faced with the rest of my life
My body is screaming no,
No this is not for me

I want to break free
From the mold of pleasing

To unpack the layers of "shoulds"
That drive my actions
And poison my life

I will no longer lay myself
At the feet of others

I will no longer feel guilt
That my existence is not
Solely for them

I felt it again last night
The grip of a panicked heart
The feeling of groundlessness
That comes when loved ones are out of reach

Despite all my energy and efforts
The classes and hours of solitude
I've hopped back on the carousel of abandonment
Listening helplessly to the familiar tunes
Blaring from 28-year-old speakers

I run between the horses and tigers
Who stare at me with glazed eyes and plastic smiles
Watching as I desperately search for a sign of life
But the spinning platform is empty and bare
As are all places our minds invent

This time, instead of throwing myself off
Into the lap of an unwilling soul
I run myself to exhaustion
And collapse on the spinning floor

I wonder how long I will be here
Sitting with these unbearable feelings
Forgetting that as the engineer of this ride
Only I can dismantle the entire thing

The pain of trying to reach myself and only meeting a solid wall settles in me like the heaviness of every brick used to build it

What if this time you stayed
What if you gave me everything I wanted
Would that make the pain go away
Or am I using you as an excuse
To distract from the black hole inside my chest
That swallows anyone who gets near
And whispers discontents in my ear
So if you don't leave, eventually I will
And because I've perfected the art of self-deception
I'm always left wondering why it failed

The room is dark and full of heavy objects
It casts long shadows into the hallway
A past neglected, calling to be examined
But I pass by without entering

I opt for more predictable spaces
Filled with ignorance and folly
At least there's lightness here
Though I often leave feeling numb

I've composed essays and charts
To explain away my absence
I hide behind intellectualism
As I hurry onto the next task

Day after day the excuse varies
But the end is always the same
Avoiding the darkness until the objects pile up
Threatening to knock down the door
And spill out onto the manicured carpet

I'm sure your story is complex
But all I saw was the cruelty
The way you brought your children to their knees
And subjected them to a life of tyranny

Your poison did not weaken with age
And you brought your prison with you
Erecting it around everyone
And infecting us with your misery

I stood over you as I grew older
Falling into a role I didn't choose
One of a protector full of rage
Defending those who lost their voice

Though now the worst of it has passed
The legacy of your abuse runs thick
We are still tearing down the walls
And learning how to breathe freely

If I could say sorry and have it mean something to you
I would apologize for the laws we lived under
For the person I was before I knew myself
But these days our lives are a thousand miles apart
And my voice would fall on the ears of a stranger
Someone who has made peace with the past
Instead of waiting for something that may never come

The fear is so potent
It could dissolve my whole body
Individual cells vibrating
As they reach for higher ground

The walls seem closer than yesterday
The faucet drips a little more frequently
I pace around the empty apartment
As if entering each room would bring back
Those who've moved on

But there is no one here but fear
A more frequent visitor these days
Inviting me to collapse on the coffee-stained carpet
And I accept
Again

Moving at high speed
My mind races the world

My body stays in one place
Though I tremble in protest

The old scripts run reliably
Saying I will lose control if I slow

So I dance faster and faster
Leaving everyone behind

Everytime I get sucked under
It feels as permanent as death

As if this riptide will not release
Until it has severed all connection

Until I can no longer reach love
Or recognize myself inside my body

And when it finally spits me out
I blink in the blinding sunlight

And swear next time I will remember
That the water eventually recedes

But when the inevitable undertow arrives
I find I've forgotten everything I learned

If my fear was a jazz band
The instruments would play out of sync
The cymbals would clash
And the bass would pluck strings off key

The guitar's notes would rattle
Because the action was a little too high
Fingers would push hard against the neck
Unable to produce clean sound

The snare would catch the rest by surprise
Jolting an already fragile arrangement
The singer would often lose its voice
And blame it on the microphone

Oh fear, how you refuse to change
How all who walk on stage with you are consumed
And as you deny theory and foundation
The audience gets up and leaves, one by one

Knotted body
Bent sideways
To avoid acknowledging
Painful emotions

But the eventual retaliation
Of a body pushed to the edge
Is far more painful
Than feeling ever is

This chest holds a brick
Where my heart used to be
Blood moves with malaise
Through veins
It once used to course

The cost of disconnection
Tolls through the body
The mind spins pointlessly
Lost in the limbo between
Logic and feeling

If we are wired to connect
Why are our systems so easily broken?
Hearts hanging on by sinew
Primed to lose everything

But would the final cut
Be any less painful
Than the torturous process
Of mending this fragile bond?

His starving hands grabbed my waist as if his loneliness would be satiated if I could just come close enough

I learned the art of papier mache early
Painstakingly dampening each layer
Spreading sadness on top of fear
And burying anger at the bottom

The structures I created were monstrous
They lurked in the corner of the bedroom
Sending shadows creeping across my bed
A constant reminder of their power over me

I wanted to throw up my hands and quit
To tear down the obstacles I planted in my path
But life had laid the supplies at my feet
And the compulsion to use them was overwhelming

I wish you had taken the stuffed animal from me
That day at the hospital
When my best idea to heal your broken body
Was to bring you a teddy bear
But your suggestion that I take it home instead
Meant that I had failed

Body slumped with dread
As the minutes tick by
My phone vibrates and I lunge
Is it you?
Will you tell me I'm valuable?
That I'm someone worth something?

But no, it's not you.

It's a friend with a funny quote
Or a sibling confirming plans
And I can't take in that love
Because my instinct is to fill myself with you
And if your thumbs pay me attention
Then maybe I'm good enough

Will the moment come when you no
longer look at me as your lover
As the fire you have fallen into
That licks your skin but doesn't burn?

And when it does, what choice will you make?
Will you take my hand and step into our next chapter
Or rip out the story and leave the embers behind?

The weight of uncertainty feels like a fallen tree
Slowly suffocating me as I shiver in the cold
Every movement only seems to make it heavier
I call out to those nearby, getting louder in my desperation

I used to trust myself to know the best thing to do
I had maps, justifications, and rationales
I could conduct lessons on the best decision
Arriving at my conclusions with confidence

But now, stripped to the bone, I'm unsure.
With my patterns reflected back at me
I can't find the right path or see the way out
And missteps lead me deeper into the wild

So my doubt keeps me rooted to the spot
Fear and confusion swirling at my feet
And as I wait for the next tree to fall
I fail to make any decision at all

The potency of fear permeates the room
As we sit one-by-one, averting our gaze
The heaviness of years lived in isolation
Weighing on minds already infected
With the thought of sickness
Even if bodies don't yet host the virus

How long can skin survive without touch?
How long can souls survive without being seen?
This distance is another kind of killer
The one that takes us out more quietly
Without cough or supplemental oxygen
Only the final faint breath expelled
From a human so utterly alone

The edges are sharp and jagged
A marker of a situation unknown
Threatening to pierce me if I come close

So I decide to stay in the middle
The flatlands where nothing happens
The place I've lived my entire life

If only I recognized the edge as a teacher
That the pain would encourage new growth
But instead I watch myself atrophy

There are so many things I want to say to you
But only if you would hear them
Only if you wouldn't look away or make a joke
So my words might touch a deeper place

The reasons for this rift boil inside me
Making me scream until my body catches fire
I lash out at everyone but you
As if others are responsible for our disconnection

I teeter between action and apathy
Afraid to push you, but more so terrified
Of one day standing at your gravestone
Wishing I had made a different choice

You are still there waiting patiently
Smiling at me through the darkness
As if my absence was not shameful

You kiss my hand and say I inspire you
That my full tilt run into the dark unknown
Helps you reach into your own mind

But fear courses deep in my veins
And I am often surprised that you stay
Continuing to hold me with love and comfort

I hope one day to believe that I'm not too much

Awakening

When I first approached these memories
It felt like I was walking to my death
With ragged breath and numb arms
My mind erecting barriers to keep me out

I saw myself standing in the shadow
Dwarfed by a towering brick wall
Whose tightly furled barbed wire
Pulsed an electric warning of my fate
Should I attempt to cross over

So I stood there watching
Fear snaking down my spine
Palms sweaty and heart pounding
The animal inside reminding me
Of all the ways I could die

When the overwhelm became too great
I turned and walked away
I would return tomorrow and the day after that
Until my body no longer screamed
Until I could calmly say I'm ready now
Please show me what lies beyond your borders

I medicate myself with you
You, the latest man in my life
I lure you in with light-hearted confidence
And once you're in love with me
I demand you be my cure

As the refills run out
I write myself a new prescription
Convinced this next drug will fix me
That a new man will take away my pain

The years tick by and I've yet to find my drug
I try generics and new formulations
I double-dose and mix and match
But each time I end up alone
Surrounded by empty bottles and broken hearts

There is one prescription I've yet to write
The one that requires nothing of anyone else
Only my own willingness to sit in the fire of my pain
To let it consume me and risk annihilation
And then rebuild a life from the ashes

Fear is my armor
It protects me from the unpredictable
It makes me work double time
So I'm never caught off guard

It's often exhausting
To run laden with the weight
But I tell myself my safety is worth it
And I know no other way

But last night my armor fell away
It cascaded off with no warning
And before I could catch it
It exposed what was living underneath

It was a grief so powerful
It dropped me to the ground
Unbound and unapologetic
Pouring deep from the well of my body

My howling cries joined other voices
Voices of the ones who came before
Whose stories still live in my skin
Those who never had a chance to feel

And as I lay curled on the ground
It was them I thought of
Grief washing over me
As I whispered: may we all be free

What if the threat passed long ago?
And only the memory of it lives on in my body
Stuck on replay, like a record I won't remove from the player
Because I'm too afraid of the silence

Consciousness flickers
Like a flame starved of oxygen
Eyelids as heavy as my heart
As I struggle for coherence

This is a year of stormy seas
And the waves aren't easily ridden
Even when I enter willingly
I meet a determined current

So I come back to these lungs
And the wonder of my breath
A chest rising and falling
Greeting one wave at a time

Some war zones only reveal themselves in the quiet

⟡

What would it be like to unclench the fist
That has become numb from the effort
From the pain of defending
A heart that was hurt so young
Would I die?

I want to go off in search of the little boy
The one who was full of love and laughter
But learned to run away from home
And seek safety in the branches of tall trees

Who might he have grown into
If he had been loved as he ought to have been?
How might he have shown up differently
If his gifts had been noticed and nurtured?

If I could find him I would wrap him in my arms
Whisper kind truths into his small ears
And help him realize his worth
To know that all of him has a right to this world

The tapestry in the back of the store hangs dusty and forgotten
Shoppers prefer the ones on display
With their pristine weaves and brightly colored patterns
Whose newness boasts of value

But I'm drawn to the one in the back
The one with tattered edges and dirty fringe
Small holes worn from uneven pressure
Where a chair leg might have sat for too many years
Stifling color and thread

What stories does this tapestry hold?
What joys and sorrows would it whisper?
Maybe ones of neglect
When after years of children playing
It was suddenly left alone
Or maybe tales of crowding
Of too many feet or too much furniture
Digging into its lungs as it struggled to breathe

These are the experiences I'm interested in
Rather than the display window in all of its sparkling superficiality
Full of tapestries who've yet to weave a history

Your body seems heavy, your eyes dull
I rarely hear you sing these days

I remember the day he arrived
A warm August breeze played through the trees
As he unloaded more than furniture from that truck

Every time you sat with him
A shadow passed across your face
You returned slower, heavier than you left
And though he once gave you life
I wondered if now he was stealing it

No one can save you
You must be brave enough, aware enough
To scoop up the child of your heart
And soothe her to safety

Oh how I've seen your strength
You are water, dammed for too long
Longing to break through
To show the world your light and power

Pick up your tools
And break down the dam

The slip into abuse was so subtle I almost didn't notice it
All I saw was how my body responded differently
How my arms went numb when you had that look in your eyes
Or how I didn't want to open my legs to you anymore

I found myself hiding feelings and conversations
Keeping them from those closest to me, including myself
So that even when I became afraid of your hands
I vowed to work harder instead of seeking help

When the end finally came and I drove away from your house
My mind clearing and my back slowly ceasing to spasm
I left behind the desperate pleas of a child clinging to her captor
And stepped into a version of myself that I did not yet know

As I adjusted to a life free from emotional captivity
I realized that I could not have taken any other path
That this test was an essential part of my story
A waypoint on my journey to self-knowledge

And all those times you yelled and swore
Your words stirred a long-forgotten piece of me
The piece with boundaries and unshakeable strength
And I realized I was no longer afraid to say no

Some experiences aren't meant to be good
But instead serve to reveal you to yourself
They show you that freedom was always there
Lying dormant, just waiting to burst forth

Do I want to shed this hardened skin
That has grown around my body?
I'm wearing it in all of my memories
But I'm beginning to realize it doesn't fit well

It squeezes me and restricts my movement
Molding me into uncomfortable shapes
So I contort myself to move through the world
Hiding behind a smile as I buckle from the pressure

But this discomfort is familiar
And if there's one thing I've learned
It's that I tend to hold onto familiar things
Even as they suffocate me

But if I dared explore what's beneath this skin
I might face a woman I don't recognize
She could be infinitely powerful
And I'm used to living in powerlessness

So I come back to the question that always leaves me paralyzed:
What if I don't know how to be free?

The redwood towers over my 6-year-old frame
Casting shadows that hint of storytelling
It gently sways in the wind, beckoning
Tempting me with its wisdom and care

My small feet crunch across the uneven ground
A bed of green needles strewn with pebbles
And soon I am embraced by the branches
Shielded from the responsibility for anyone but myself

My hands reach out and I hoist myself into the air
The furry bark is soft under my bare feet as I climb
Breathing in the scent of damp earth
As my limbs work rhythmically
To carry my small body upwards

I perch on a sturdy branch somewhere near the top
The view is beautiful, but I don't look at it
Because I haven't come here for beauty
I've come here for peace

I've come to be held by something much older than me
To lean against the trunk and breathe deeply
And as I let fear sink into roots buried deep underground
The earth reminds me that she will be there
Waiting to care for me just as I am

You reached out to the world tonight
Hoping for answers to new questions
Hands trembling, you dried your palms
As you stared at the boxes on the screen

But time rushed forward with indecent haste
And you were not invited to share
No one could know it was the first time
You decided to risk using your voice

My dear there will come a time soon
When you won't need to rehearse
Your body will not sweat or shake
Or perceive a threat to its own survival

Instead your voice will be clear and strong
You will speak from that place deep inside
That has always known worth and wisdom
And you will allow yourself to be witnessed

The nest you built was comfortable and safe
I took refuge in it when I felt scared
Some days I would refuse to leave
Though my kin had long since flown away

Sometimes I would wait patiently for your return
But most times I cried out in fear
You tended to my needs so expertly
That I never tried to take care of them myself

I would tremble among the familiar twigs
Praying that nothing would make me move
That I would never have to face the harshness of the world
And you would take care of me forever

But death and change are reliable friends
And it is time I stretched my wings
It is time to plummet to the ground
So I can finally learn how to fly

The brushstrokes on my skin are new and much too shiny
I shield my eyes in front of their colorful brilliance

I'm told I will soon begin to recognize them as my own
That these parts of me have always been there
And are surfacing because of the sloughing off of old ways

But like trying on a beautiful new dress
That I'm sure is meant for someone else
The change in the mirror makes me cringe

How do I embrace this canvas full of color
When I've never been free to paint with my whole palette?

It takes courage to reach for the sky instead of settling yourself against the warmest wall of the well and believing there is no way out

When I get close to new depth
My mind shuts itself down
It puts me to sleep
Rather than risk the change
That often accompanies epiphany

Choosing something different is painful
Like a caterpillar spinning the cocoon
In which it must decay
I struggle against my dissolution

My body yearns for familiarity
While my mind justifies old patterns
Anything to distract from facing the knowledge
That I must facilitate my own transformation

So I pick up my fear
And wrap myself in silk
Though the process may be uncomfortable
It's time to greet my new form

If I were to count the parts of me
That often run the show
I'd see a few familiar faces
Jumping into the driver's seat

Most are nervous and impossibly young
Trying to career the vehicle to safety
Taking out poles, trees, and other people
Doing their best to survive

The part of me that should be driving
Has long been pushed away
She failed in a crucial moment
And is no longer trusted to lead

It took me coming to my own rescue
After I had crashed too many times
To finally visit the orphanage inside
And begin to get to know myself

Now they are starting to trust
Given evidence of my competence
These parts are slowly releasing their roles
Once again free to play as children

Raging, sobbing, cowering in fear
I practice these states of being so often
That when they occur naturally
I do not sink into shame or suppression

These sessions give me a blueprint
They show me how to find my balance
When my mind flees to the past
In pursuit of artificial safety measures

And through this practice I'm learning
That awareness is not enough
True health means an active relationship
With all that arises in my internal life

Would I scold a child
If she came to me with her fears?
Would I say, "Not this again"
Or "Why can't you feel less?"

Yet I police the pieces of me
That are not yet healed
I wish that they were different
And I say this to their face

But I've been around long enough to know
That judgment does not lend itself to freedom
Only love creates enough safety
To feel what is trapped inside

The mind that learns to observe itself is no longer beholden to unconscious patterning

I recognize myself in you
The breaking and growth
The desire to survive
The need to deconstruct my knotted limbs

And that is only what is seen
Below the surface
My roots grow deep, like yours
Seemingly forgotten, yet the foundation for which I grow
I am only beginning to appreciate the importance of the
expedition underground

Hello little one
Come here and let me wipe your tears
Let me stroke your hair and soothe your fears
While you honor me with the gift of your words

Your wails pierce me to the bone
I hear the need behind the rage and fear
The desperate sound of a child trying to survive
Flailing body in search of solid ground

I know you don't yet trust me
But I promise I got here as soon as I could
So I'll sit with an open lap and an open heart
Until you believe I'm here to stay

Practicing alone is never the same
As being faced with a real situation
Unfolding, rapidly

Like a gunman crouched in a trench
Trying to avoid the enemy
I look at you, frozen

Words don't come out right
There's no hope of harmony
I'm closed, distant

I try not to be discouraged
Because at least now I notice
I've left, again

I notice access to myself is cut off
And I can make the choice to shift
To step away, for now

I return when my body feels safe
And can speak from a place of connection
So we can heal, together

Last night I dreamt you died
But unlike normal dreams
Where I wake up with a shock
It continued on for hours
My heart breaking with grief
The pain searing through me
As I uttered animalistic cries
Clawing at the ground
Unable to reach you

When I woke I realized you were alive
Though the feelings lingered
Their intensity pulsing through me
So I knelt on my floor at dawn
And wet the carpet with my tears
Honoring my mind's latest lesson

Because what I think happened that night
Is the release of the part of me
That so wholly depends on you
It tricks me into thinking I would die too
If anything were to happen to you

So I wait for the waves to finish crashing
Before I dry my tears and stand up
I wrap myself in my arms
And whisper words of comfort
Reminding myself that I am strong
And that my system is learning the art
Of unraveling of old ways

Out, out
Climb out of my body
Out from the deep well
You've lived your whole life

Reach towards the light
Where you might be seen
Bring your howls and rage
And let me be your witness

Holding the whole world
In this one mind
Is enough to bring
Anyone to the ground
Kneeling in the grass
Praying to a god
We don't believe in

Grief calls us to recognize
That which is beyond ourselves
To tear down the facade
Of humanity living siloed
Apart from all the rest

There is beauty here
In the collapse
The surrender
To our dependence
On this earth
And her suffering

Beauty in her rage
As she tips back
Towards balance
Reminding us
Of our own fragility

Ignorance is not an excuse for cruelty
But rather a call for education
To learn more about one's own heart
In order to free others of our pain

There is a place in the shadows
Where suffering souls meet
A clubhouse whose membership
Hosts the lonely and ashamed

An old woman crouched in the corner
Who has never been enough for herself
A young boy wailing loudly
Whose unmet needs consume him

Living in this world means
We all meet here eventually
The darkness will pull us in
And convince us we are alone

So next time you find yourself
Deep in the trenches of your own despair
Pause to notice nearby faces
Feel the relief of holding others' pain
And revel in the remedy of belonging

These pages help me breathe
They give language to the life living inside
The changing animal of my mind can be seen
In all of its evolving imperfections

Self-witnessing opens up new plains
Where birds soar and sing
The sky is the deepest blue
And the warm wind tastes like freedom

Except when it doesn't
Because witnessing means seeing what you don't like
Walking barefoot on a ground of injury and decay
Trudging through shame and self-loathing

I am rendered raw from this rebirth
So for now,
I soothe the wounds with words

I've never met a more ardent teacher than my own grief

The last time I visited, you called me a stranger
There was no recognition or warm welcome
It was almost as if you expected me not to return

I suppose I deserved the treatment
I had been away much too long
Busy neglecting my promises to you

I'm sorry for the length of my absence
But I will sit here with your cold indifference
And wait for you to gift me with your trust

Nostalgia settles over me
As I analyze my happiness
A feeling so foreign and unfamiliar
That I begin to ache for the chaos of the past
Because at least I knew how to be in pain

Your kind eyes invite my words
And though my hands shake
Fear stirring in my belly
I accept the gift of your ears

My trembling voice echoes
Hot pinpricks coat my arms
But still I speak on
Leaning into your warmth

I introduce you to the parts
That for so long I pushed away
The ugly, imperfect pieces
I swore never to reveal

But something is different this time
The fear is muted, gray
A spectator in the crowd
Watching wisdom take center stage

And when you wrap me in your arms
Your love sits neatly on top of mine
I no longer need to drink it down
Like a lost child dying of thirst

For I've quenched this need myself
And now we can walk side by side
Two whole and separate beings
Both curious to see what comes next

I saw her again last night
The woman with the confident laugh

I watched from a distance as she talked passionately
Drawing in those sitting closeby with her easy smile

Each moment of the dinner unfolded seamlessly
As she danced her way through the conversation

And when she got up to leave, she faced me
And it was then that I understood

One day soon I would not see the separation
But look through her eyes and realize we are one

Healing

Remember when we collected stickers
from the bowling alley?
With our glitter eyeshadow and spaghetti strap tops
Using both hands to roll a ball down bumpered lanes
Devouring cheese pizza and licking the grease from our fingers

In those days I didn't know I was fragmenting
That the screaming in my head was not a phase
I just learned how to hide it better as I grew older
How to smile at adults and say everything is okay

I never questioned my way of being
And assumed my best was good enough
That decorating the prison wall
Was the same freedom as having the key

So I wondered why my relationships withered
Why my efforts always came up short
It took falling into the darkest of places
To start the work of excavating my own mind

The road to healing has been long and mostly dark
The shadows hide potholes and sharp branches
I've fallen and wished the earth would absorb my body
But I always end up back on my feet trudging forward

It's been twenty years and I want to go bowling again
I want to forget the words trauma, fear, and anger
So I'll meet you in the center of town with quarters in my pocket
And we can bury our hands in popcorn and cheer as the pins fall

The maple glows red with the turning of the season
Fluttering in the slight breeze that tickles its leaves

The rooster's crow breaks the sleepy silence
Serenading branches of lichen-draped redwoods
As they undulate like wooden pendulums

They keep their own interpretation of time
Reminding us to pause and breathe

For the natural world offers many lessons
If only we would slow down enough to listen

I love when events are linear
Because when they follow a line
They become predictable
They are easier to understand
To evaluate and anticipate

But healing doesn't work this way
Believe me I've tried to make it so
I've set up timelines and graphs
And berated myself for missing
Countless made up milestones

Instead the answer is
What no one wants to hear
That the process is a mystery
To which you can only surrender

Progress can't be defined by the mind
Only as a deep internal shift
Subtle, abrupt, slow, or accelerated
It presents in unexpected forms

So leave the mind to its business
Of churning out new predictions
Drop down into the body
And listen to the deeper knowing
That has always lived in your bones

I tried to create a space without edges
Free from judgment and sharp tongues
So I could move through it safely
Avoiding the discomfort of fear and anger

Anyone who wished to enter
Was screened fiercely at the door
Take off your shoes and soften your words
There's only room for my version of you here

The safety I thought I was building
Took constant vigilance to maintain
I told myself that exhaustion
Was a worthy trade for survival

But my world became small
And those who entered quickly left
I watched the discomfort creep in anyways
Growing relentlessly until it forced me to change

So I shed my conditions and rulebooks
And stepped into a world I thought would destroy me
But my words still flow to the page
And I've learned that venturing into the wild unknown
Is better than remaining in the broken familiar

The resistance to healing is strong
It uses myriad strategies to enact its agenda
It is subtle, loud, practical, and cunning
As it tries to pull me from the work
Convince me that the status quo is the way
To deliver the relief I've been seeking

But the longer I sit in the stillness of my mind
The easier it is to see the players
I don't go to war with them much anymore
Afterall, I would only be fighting myself
Engaging in a battle that has no winners
For they too are a part of me
With an equal right to be heard

How many more times
Must my heart break open
Before I realize it is never truly damaged?

Each time I pick up the pieces
And put them back together
It reveals a different and more beautiful form

Yet I am always surprised
To see it shatter once again
And convince myself that I am irredeemable

But this fear proves false
And the delicate kintsugi of my heart
Only increases my capacity to love

I thought liberation would come all at once
Bursting onto the scene in all its light and glory
But I'm learning that liberation is a quieter presence
Sneaking in the back door when you are busy working
Settling into a chair, waiting to be noticed

Liberation shows up to my house cautiously
Ready to step out as soon as it is required to stay
It leaves without a promise of when it will return
Preferring steady absence to desperate demands

So I neaten my house the best I can
And make space for the clutter I can't clear
Knowing that when my guest arrives
She will sit among it all and smile

Thoughts coat the mind
As ocean froth covers sand
The waves recede
Turning white sand dark
But this time it sparkles

Waves can appear ferocious
Pounding the shore
As if determined to hurt it
Other times they glide smoothly
Kissing the sand in perfect harmony

The nature of change is constant
At least I can rely on that
This unyielding energy
Creates both waves and thoughts
And it carries no agenda

Pain is our own interpretation
Of this energy's intent
And it can render neutrality
As happiness or hell

The words to a poem about peace
Are disjointed and slow moving
They do not flow like the river of painful ones
But still they form and try to break free

They mirror the internal landscape
Where peace has just begun to take root
And the tender saplings reach for the light
In hopes they can weather the next storm

Maybe one day these trees will be taller than the others
And they will smile down on all that came before
Peace will draw strength from the roots of early pain
And treasure the diversity of the forest

There will be times we want to turn away
To flee from our minds and bodies
Like an animal escaping the hunter's trap
We think we can avoid the pain of feeling

Yet despite our own convictions
Turning towards the difficult and distressing
The feelings that repulse or frighten us
Does not make them larger or more in control

It will instead reveal the soft underbelly
Of a part of us needing care
Curling up and wishing to be hugged
Or screaming out and wishing to be heard

For what is love if not the gift of our attention?

I try to remember that the storm will pass
And when morning arrives with clear skies in tow
I will survey the landscape outside my window
Fresh dew clinging to tender grass
Air crisp like the first apple of the season
And breathe out the shadows and the fear

His voice echoed from far away
Unknowingly, blissfully
I had drifted down a hallway
Into a room full of tantalizing distraction
But his words were a gentle tether
Inviting me back to the moment
And with one more breath I arrived
Back to my only true home

Trusting myself turned out to be the most natural thing I have ever been brave enough to try

There are those days when my storylines are proven false
When my persistent beliefs are shown to have no weight

Sometimes the news comes all at once
As if speed has a hand in driving toxic thoughts out

And the new thoughts rush in
Ones that bring me to my knees
That write new stories that start with maybe

Maybe I'm smart
Maybe I'm worthy
Maybe I'm enough just as I am

I never realized I had shattered into pieces
That the fragments had their own thoughts and will
Instead I thought I was unstable and irrational
Someone to keep under lock and key
So as not to betray my brokenness in public

The pieces didn't seem to fit together
Some had jagged edges and others ran away
So I desperately tried to corral them all
To squeeze them together into one
As if that would make me whole

But the more forceful my hand
As I sought to control rather than observe
The more quickly they disappeared
Taking refuge in the recesses of my mind
Behind walls they erected to keep me out

Though now I've learned to greet them
To invite each one to the table
So they may share their fear and anger
Still sometimes I slip into judgment
Thinking their absence would bring me peace

But this trust was not easily built
So I show up again and again
As the patient steward of my mind
So I might bring balance to the system

Those who are threatened by your journey are only reflecting their own fear of themselves

Your project looms large in the room
A dismantled frame suspended in mid-air
Orphaned parts pile high on the floor
Leaving the appearance of disarray

Yet to know the full story
Is to realize this is an evolution
A journey of transformation
To become something stronger than before

So it waits patiently by the window
Light dancing off an alloyed body
Knowing change will arrive swiftly
To reveal the final form

Learning to trust myself meant I didn't need everyone to behave exactly right
I didn't need to know what the parking lot looked like before I got in the car
Or who was calling before I picked up the phone

Instead I raised my hand in a room of a hundred people
I allowed myself to say I don't know, but I will get back to you
Learning to trust myself meant releasing others from the burden of my burdens

I feel my back stiff and tight in the mornings
I roll clumsily out of bed
Moving gingerly across the room
So as not to exacerbate the pain

The classic explanations are meaningless
I've lived in this body long enough to know that
Instead I've learned to treat pain as a messenger
Bringing forth news from my unconscious mind

I place a hand on my back and close my eyes
What are you trying to tell me?
My mind sits with the pain and patiently waits
As deep listening inevitably forms connection

And the sadness rises from a deep well in my body
Spilling out like a tide pouring over a seawall
I brace myself against the floor as sobs rack my chest
And give myself over to the wisdom of release

When the flow ebbs and I've mopped my tears
I thank my body for showing me what we needed
For now the tension is less under my fingers
And it will let me know when there is more to say

When the tea is drunk
The dishes are cleaned
And the laundry is folded
I sit alone in the silence
Letting my thoughts wash over me

I remember when I used to fear them
When I believed their content was true
The manipulation would eat my insides away
Leaving nothing but scraps of tissue and bone
Splayed open and waiting for the vultures

I turned myself inside out back then
Contorting into shapes and donning fake smiles
Just to make it through another day
An 8-year-old so afraid of herself
That she cried to her mother to lock her up

If I could talk to that little girl I would say
That sometimes life is painful and scary
But like the weather in the sky, it will pass

I would stroke her hair and tell her
Thoughts are harmless and impersonal
That fear is not bad nor will it consume you
If you can sit and feel it you will begin to heal it

These days I watch my thoughts go by
Their energy, content, and how they feel in my body
Am I tight or loose, closed or open?
And as the decades pass and the wrinkles form
I find I'm trending towards peace

Joy and heartbreak
Are inseparable pieces
Of a life lived in full color

It's only now occurring to me
That I might deserve the space I take up
But my mind, ravaged by fear and doubt
Tricked me into staying small
Until I could no longer breathe
And it wasn't until I broke open
That I realized I was enough all along

I had to run off the edge of a cliff to learn that the universe would catch me

There is no world in which berating ourselves into healing brings forth authentic change. Only love and acceptance disarms us enough for true transformation to take place

This time I'm not begging you to stay
Before you've considered leaving
I'm not strategizing
And calculating
Or losing myself in plans
Because when I look into your eyes
My body is quiet
And it's there that I can hear the truth
That true safety is not having the perfect road map
It is not the declaration of promises
Or everlasting love
It is standing next to you in the moonlight,
Not knowing, together

Remember those days you thought you couldn't do it
When I held your head up for you?
Remember the slog through the seemingly endless plains
When you thought there was no hope left?

I saw your strength and drive, your desperate will to survive
I saw your light, dimmed by a thousand doubts and fears
Waiting for the moment to burn as brightly as it was meant to

And look at you now, shining from the mountaintop
Illuminating everyone around you

Your gaze tethers me to the moment
Breath catches in my throat
I feel an upswell of love and safety
Like warm bath water reaching up
To envelop me in its comfort
Your hand caresses my cheek, my hair
And the touch feels like home

An unfamiliar confidence has crept into my life
And I notice my body more at ease these days

It's not the boastful kind that masks insecurity
But a quiet kind that tells me I'm okay
That the winds may rage around me
But I have what I need to weather the storm

Most times I don't notice it's there
But then I see myself taking risks
Or staying calm in the face of the usual triggers
And I wonder where the fear has gone

I thought there would be more fireworks
A switch flipped to announce my evolution
Instead there is a subtle thread
Weaving together a balanced mind

And while the work has been plenty
I know that new hardships will come
But for now the quiet is enough
So I sip my tea and smile

I'd like to see you look at me like that more often
As if I were the adventure you were seeking
As if I could take on the world, with or without you
Who knows, I probably could

Out beyond fields of gold
Next to the lush green flora
Fed by a gently flowing river
There is a place full of light

The sun shines brightly here
Flitting between tall trees
Bathing colorful flowers
That spring from soft earth

I've visited twice in my life
When I didn't know who I was
A prerequisite to entry
It is a fleeting unlearning

I danced between the ferns
And tasted freedom in the berries
I picked up my guitar and strummed
A melody so beautiful I weeped

What a relief it is
To forget all the stories
To release ourselves from judgment
And just be with what is

The only thing not welcome here
Is that which we bring with us
It is stripped away at the gate
Leaving only an unbound soul

I will work a lifetime for just one more glimpse

When I breathe in the free air
I know that I am unstoppable

I want to roar from the rooftops
All that I have been through
All that I have seen
To tell the world that peace is possible

That journeying through the darkness is worth it

X marks a body
Thought to be untarnished
Like the glassy surface
Of a lake at rest

Yet we were never blank
Slates to be written upon
For even birth is traumatic
And by now we are covered

Scars of the body
Indicate the finite
A start and an end
An event from this lifetime

Scars of the mind
Hold a longer history
The story and the weight
Of not being asked about it

Who will be brave enough
To reopen generations
Of wounds improperly healed
Waiting to bleed, to be freed?

About the Author

Malena Spar has been exploring her mind and the world around her through meditation, dreamwork, and psychotherapy for over a decade. Born and raised in Northern California, she is a firm believer in surfacing what we usually bury, the mind's ability to change, and the power of healing in community.

www.ingramcontent.com/pod-product-compliance
Lightning Source LLC
Chambersburg PA
CBHW020424130626